$$\left[\begin{array}{c} \text{Q U O T A B L E} \\ \text{W I S D O M} \end{array} \right]$$

●

Mother Teresa

Edited by
CAROL KELLY-GANGI

FALL RIVER PRESS

New York

FALL RIVER PRESS

New York

An Imprint of Sterling Publishing
387 Park Avenue South
New York, NY 10016

Compilation © 2014 by Fall River Press
Originally published in 2006 as *Mother Teresa: Her Essential Wisdom*.

ISBN 978-1-4549-1120-3

Distributed in Canada by Sterling Publishing
c/o Canadian Manda Group, 165 Dufferin Street
Toronto, Ontario, Canada M6K 3H6
Distributed in the United Kingdom by GMC Distribution Services
Castle Place, 166 High Street, Lewes, East Sussex, England BN7 1XU
Distributed in Australia by Capricorn Link (Australia) Pty. Ltd.
P.O. Box 704, Windsor, NSW 2756, Australia

For information about custom editions, special sales, and premium and
corporate purchases, please contact Sterling Special Sales at 800-805-5489
or specialsales@sterlingpublishing.com.

Manufactured in the United States of America

6 8 10 9 7 5

www.sterlingpublishing.com

Table of Contents

Introduction vii

A Call to Serve 1
God the Father, the Son, and the Holy Spirit 11
Love 15
Charity 19
The Poor and Poverty 27
Family Life 35
Peace in the World 41
Speaking to Youth 45
Prayer, Faith, and Holiness 51
Humility 61
Chastity 67
Joy 71
The Blessed Mother 77
The Gift of Life 83
Suffering and Death 89
Sin and Forgiveness 95
Money 99
Religion 103
Women 109
The Religious Life 113
Remembering Mother Teresa 121

Chronology 129

To my sister Marianne with love—
for your lifetime of giving.

Introduction

M OTHER TERESA WAS TRAVELING on a train in Darjeeling, India, on September 10, 1946, when she heard the voice of God. The message she received would prove to be life-altering not only for her, but for millions of people all over the world. God's message was clear and undeniable: Go live and work among the poorest of the poor.

She was born Agnes Gonxha Bojaxhiu on August 27, 1910, in Skopje, present-day Macedonia, the youngest of descent. Despite her father's death when she was only nine, Agnes enjoyed a happy childhood and was very involved with activities at the neighboring church, the Sacred Heart of Jesus. At the age of twelve, Agnes felt the beginnings of a call to the religious life. Though Agnes's mother was initially against the idea of her beloved Agnes leaving home to become a sister, she later understood that this was her daughter's calling, and prophetically advised Agnes, "Put your hand in His hand and walk all alone with Him."

In 1928, Agnes became a novitiate in the Sisters of Our Lady of Loreto, an Irish order that ran missionary schools in India. After a brief period of training in Dublin, Agnes set out for India, and in 1931, after two years as a novice, Agnes professed her temporary vows and chose the name Teresa, after St. Thérèse of Lisieux, the patron saint of missionaries. For the next seventeen years, Sister Teresa lived in Calcutta and taught at St. Mary's High School, a school attended by largely middle-class girls. She professed her final vows as a Sister of Loreto, and ultimately became the director of studies at St. Mary's. She loved teaching, and claimed that at Loreto, she was the "happiest nun in the world."

Mother Teresa later revealed that the decision to leave Loreto was her greatest sacrifice, and the hardest thing she had ever done. Yet, she vowed to follow what she believed was God's will for her, her "call within a calling," and, in 1948, after receiving permission from Rome, she left the Sisters of Loreto for the slums of Calcutta. She took a three-month course in medical care, and opened a school for children of the poor. One by one, a small number of her former students joined Mother Teresa, and in 1950, the Order of Missionaries of Charity was authorized by Rome. In 1952, Mother Teresa opened a home for the dying, followed the next year by her first orphanage.

At the heart of Mother Teresa's ministry was her deeply held belief that everything she did, she did for the love of God. It was not the broken, dying bodies of the poor that she and her sisters attended to, but rather, to Jesus himself, coming to them in the distressing disguise of the poor. She firmly believed that in order to understand the life of the poor, she and her sisters must choose a life of poverty for themselves, and strive toward ever greater humility, all in an effort to fulfill the vow of the Missionaries of Charity to joyfully give "wholehearted and free service to the poorest of the poor." She won numerous awards for her work, including the Nobel Peace Prize in 1979, which she accepted in the name of the poor and unloved everywhere.

Despite critics who questioned her staunch beliefs against abortion and birth control, and those who claimed that she did not question the sources of donations, Mother Teresa remained undaunted, choosing to accept criticism with a smile and go on about her work.

What Mother Teresa began with a handful of members has grown to an order that is active in more than 130 countries, running a worldwide network of shelters for the poor and homeless, orphanages, AIDS hospices, clinics for lepers, homes for unwed mothers, and other places of charity.

This book offers readers hundreds of inspiring quotations from Mother Teresa. In the half-century of her public life, she visited and spoke in more than one hundred countries about the subjects closest to her heart. The selections gathered here, drawn largely from her spoken words, are both simple and profound in their wisdom and truth. She speaks passionately and unflinchingly about the meaning of love, the importance of charity, the need for prayer, the value of family, the role of suffering, and the absolute dignity of every human being. She also reflects upon her own calling to the religious life, and her calling to devote her life to serve the poorest of the poor.

At the age of eighty-seven, Mother Teresa died and was mourned the world over. More than 15,000 people attended her funeral, and a million or more crowded the streets of Calcutta to pay their respects to a woman hailed by many as a living saint. In fitting tribute to her life, dignitaries from many countries attended her funeral Mass together with many of the poor people that she had so selflessly served for more than five decades.

Mother Teresa's mission to serve the poor and unwanted of the world was fueled completely by her undying love of God. She remained deeply anchored to her faith to the end of her life, and described her place in the world with characteristic humility: "I am Albanian by birth. Now I am a citizen of India. I am also a Catholic nun. In my work, I belong to the whole world. But in my heart, I belong to Christ."

—Carol Kelly-Gangi

A Call to Serve

I was expecting to be free, but God has his own plans.

—Mother Teresa's words when her sisters
persuaded her to withdraw
her resignation, 1990

God loves me. I'm not here just to fill a place, just to be a number. He has chosen me for a purpose. I know it.

I knew that God wanted something from me. I was only twelve years old, living with my parents in Skopje, Yugoslavia (now Macedonia), when I first sensed the desire to become a nun. At that time there were some very good priests who helped boys and girls follow their vocation, according to God's call. It was then that I realized that my call was to the poor.

I remember when I was leaving home fifty years ago—my mother was dead set against me leaving home and becoming a sister. In the end, when she realized that this was what God wanted from her and from me, she said something very strange: "Put your hand in his hand and walk all alone with him." This is exactly our way of life. We may be surrounded by many people, yet our vocation is really lived out alone with Jesus.

I did my novitiate in Darjeeling and took the vows with the Loreto Sisters. For twenty years, I was at work in education in the St. Mary's High School, which was mostly for middle class children. I loved teaching, and in Loreto I was the happiest nun in the world.

In 1948, twenty years after I came to India, I actually decided upon this close contact with the poorest of the poor. It was for me a special vocation to give all to belong to Jesus. I felt that God wanted from me something more. He wanted me to be poor with the poor and to love him in the distressing disguise of the poorest of the poor. I had the blessing of obedience.

I was traveling by train to Darjeeling when I heard the voice of God. I was sure it was God's voice. I was certain he was calling me. The message was clear. I must leave the convent to help the poor by living among them. This was a command, something to be done, something definite. The call was something between God and me. What matters is that God calls each of us in a different way. In those difficult, dramatic days I was certain that this was God's doing and not mine and I am still certain. And it was the work of God. I knew that the world would benefit from it.

To leave Loreto was my greatest sacrifice, the most difficult thing I have ever done. It was much more difficult than to leave my family and country to enter religious life. Loreto meant everything to me. In Loreto I had received my spiritual training. I had become a religious there. I had given myself to Jesus in the Institute. I liked the work, teaching the girls.

On my first trip along the streets of Calcutta after leaving the Sisters of Loreto, a priest came up to me. He asked me to give a contribution to a collection for the Catholic press. I had left with five rupees, and I had given four of them to the poor. I hesitated, then gave the priest the one that remained. That afternoon, the same priest came to see me and brought an envelope. He told me that a man had given him the envelope because he had heard about my projects and wanted to help me. There were fifty rupees in the envelope. I had the feeling, at that moment, that God had begun to bless the work and would never abandon me.

One by one, from 1949 on, my former students began to arrive. They wanted to give everything to God, right away. With what joy they put away their colorful saris in order to put on our poor cotton one. They came because they knew that it would be hard. When a young woman of high caste comes and puts herself at the service of the poor, she is the protagonist of a revolution. It is the greatest, the most difficult revolution—the revolution of love.

If someone feels that God wants from him a transformation of social structures, that's an issue between him and his God. We all have the duty to serve God where we feel called. I feel called to help individuals, to love each human being. I never think in terms of crowds in general but in terms of persons. Were I to think about crowds, I would never begin anything. It is the person that matters. I believe in person-to-person encounters.

In the world there are some who struggle for justice and human rights. We have no time for this because we are in daily and continuous contact with men who are starving for a piece of bread to put in their mouth and for some affection. Should I devote myself to struggle for the justice of tomorrow or even for the justice of today, the most needy people would die right in front of me because they lack a glass of milk. . . . I do not condemn those who struggle for justice. I believe there are different options for the people of God. To me the most important is to serve the neediest people.

The reason I was given the Nobel Prize was because of the poor. However, the prize went beyond appearances. In fact, it awakened consciences in favor of the poor all over the world. It became a sort of reminder that the poor are our brothers and sisters and that we have the duty to treat them with love.

One of the most demanding things for me is traveling with all the publicity everywhere I go. I have said to Jesus if I don't go to Heaven for anything else, I will be going to Heaven for all the traveling and publicity, because it has purified me and sanctified me and made me truly ready for Heaven.

When you look at the inner workings of electrical things, you often see small and big wires, new and old, cheap and expensive, all lined up. Until the current passes through them there will be no light. That wire is you and me. The current is God. We have the power to let the current pass through us, use us, produce the light of the world. Or we can refuse to be used and allow darkness to spread.

If I had to start all over again, I would do the same thing. I have experienced many human weaknesses, many human frailties, and I still experience them. But we need to use them. We need to work for Christ with a humble heart, with the humility of Christ. He comes and uses us to be his love and compassion in the world in spite of our weaknesses and frailties.

We must know exactly when we say yes to God what is in that yes. Yes means "I surrender," totally, fully, without any counting the cost, without any examination: "Is it all right? Is it convenient?" Our yes to God is without any reservations.

I am Albanian by birth. Now I am a citizen of India. I am also a Catholic nun. In my work, I belong to the whole world. But in my heart, I belong to Christ.

God the Father, the Son, and the Holy Spirit

In God we live and move and have our being. It is God who gives life to all, who gives power and being to all that exists. But for his sustaining presence, all things would cease to be and fall back into nothingness. Consider that you are in God, surrounded and encompassed by God, swimming in God.

God dwells in us. It doesn't matter where you are as long as you are clean of heart. Clean of heart means openness, that complete freedom, that detachment that allows you to love God without hindrance, without obstacles. When sin comes into our lives that is a personal obstacle between us and God. Sin is nothing but slavery.

I can understand the greatness of God but I cannot understand his humility. It becomes so clear in him being in love with each one of us separately and completely. It is as if there is no one but me in the world. He loves me so much. Each one of us can say this with great conviction.

Do we believe that God's love is infinitely more powerful, his mercy more tender than the evil of sin, than all the hatred, conflicts, and tensions that are dividing the world? Than the most powerful bombs and guns ever made by human hands and minds?

Don't allow anything to interfere with your love for Jesus. You belong to him. Nothing can separate you from him. That one sentence is important to remember. He will be your joy, your strength. If you hold onto that sentence, temptations and difficulties will come, but nothing will break you. Remember, you have been created for great things.

Don't search for Jesus in far lands—he is not there. He is close to you; he is with you. Just keep the lamp burning and you will always see him. Keep on filling the lamp with all these little drops of love, and you will see how sweet is the Lord you love.

We are able to go through the most terrible places fearlessly, because Jesus in us will never deceive us; Jesus in us is our love, our strength, our joy, and our compassion.

Jesus loved us to the end, to the very limit, dying on the cross. We must have this same love which comes from within, from our union with Christ. Such love must be as normal to us as living and breathing.

Come, O blessed Spirit of knowledge and light, and grant that I may perceive the will of the Father. Show me the nothingness of earthly things, that I may realize their vanity and use them only for your glory and my own salvation, looking ever beyond them to you and your eternal reward.

Breathe in me, O Holy Spirit, that my thoughts may
    all be holy.
Act in me, O Holy Spirit, that my work, too, may
    be holy.
Draw my heart, O Holy Spirit, that I love but what
    is holy.
Strengthen me, O Holy Spirit, to defend all that
    is holy.
Guard me then, O Holy Spirit, that I always may
    be holy.
Amen.

Love

Love has no other message but its own. Every day we try to live out Christ's love in a very tangible way, in every one of our deeds. If we do any preaching, it is done with deeds, not with words. That is our witness to the gospel.

Let us not be afraid to be humble, small, helpless to prove our love for God. The cup of water you give the sick, the way you lift a dying man, the way you feed a baby, the way you teach a dull child, the way you give medicine to a sufferer of leprosy, the joy with which you smile at your own at home—all this is God's love in the world today.

We have to love until it hurts. It is not enough to say, "I love." We must put that love into a living action. And how do we do that? By giving until it hurts.

True love causes pain. Jesus, in order to give us the proof of his love, died on the cross. A mother, in order to give birth to her baby, has to suffer. If you really love one another, you will not be able to avoid making sacrifices.

Love is, just like Christ himself showed with his death, the greatest gift.

Love is not patronizing and charity isn't about pity, it is about love. Charity and love are the same—with charity you give love, so don't just give money but reach out your hand instead.

I try to give to the poor people for love what the rich could get for money. I wouldn't touch a leper for a thousand pounds. Yet I willingly cure him for the love of God.

As you grow, you have still to learn. I'm still learning though I am fifty-three years in the convent. I am learning from you. We have to learn from each other. Jesus took a little child and put him in front of the apostles. Love begins here. That little kindness, care, compassion, that is the hidden treasure, the growth in holiness. We know where it is, let us go for it!

The words of Jesus, "Love one another as I have loved you," must be not only a light for us but a flame that consumes the self in us. Love, in order to survive, must be nourished by sacrifices, especially the sacrifice of self.

We should ask ourselves, "Have I really experienced the joy of loving?" True love is love that causes us pain, that hurts, and yet brings us joy. That is why we must pray and ask for the courage to love.

Love is a fruit, in season at all times and within the reach of every hand. Anyone may gather it and no limit is set. Everyone can reach this love through meditation, the spirit of prayer, and sacrifice.

And so let us always meet each other with a smile, for the smile is the beginning of love, and once we begin to love each other, naturally we want to do something.

Charity

I see God in every human being. When I wash the leper's wounds I feel I am nursing the Lord himself. Is it not a beautiful experience?

Once we take our eyes away from ourselves, from our interests, from our own rights, privileges, ambitions—then they will become clear to see Jesus around us.

We Missionaries of Charity take a special vow to God to give whole-hearted, free service to the poorest of the poor. We have no income, no church assistance, no government salary, no government grants. We have none of that. And yet we deal with thousands and thousands and thousands of people, and we have never had to say to anybody, "We're sorry, we have run out of supplies."

Sometime back, a high government official said, "You are doing social work and we also are doing the same. But we are doing it for something and you are doing it for somebody." To do our work, we have to be in love with God.

I always repeat that we Missionaries of Charity are not social workers. We may be doing social work, but we are really contemplatives right at the heart of the world. We are with Jesus twenty-four hours a day. We do everything for Jesus. We do it to Jesus.

To smile at someone who is sad; to visit, even for a little while, someone who is lonely; to give someone shelter from the rain with our umbrella; to read something for someone who is blind: these and others can be small things, very small things, but they are appropriate to give our love of God concrete expression to the poor.

There are many people who can do big things, but there are very few people who will do the small things.

A beggar one day came up to me and said, "Mother Teresa, everybody gives you things for the poor. I also want to give you something. But today, I am only able to get ten pence. I want to give that to you." I said to myself, "If I take it, he might have to go to bed without eating. If I don't take it, I will hurt him." So I took it. And I've never seen so much joy on anybody's face who has given his money or food, as I saw on that man's face. He was happy that he too could give something. This is the joy of loving.

Even if you write a letter for a blind man, or you just sit and listen to someone, or you take the mail for him, or you visit somebody or bring a flower to somebody, or wash clothes for somebody or clean the house—small things, but God sees everything great.

Charity begins today. Today somebody is suffering, today somebody is in the street, today somebody is hungry. Our work is for today, yesterday has gone, tomorrow has not yet come. We have only today to make Jesus known, loved, served, fed, clothed, sheltered. Do not wait for tomorrow. Tomorrow we will not have them if we do not feed them today.

I ask you one thing: do not tire of giving, but do not give your leftovers. Give until it hurts, until you feel the pain.

The very fact that God has placed a certain soul in our way is a sign that God wants us to do something for him or her. It is not chance; it has been planned by God. We are bound by conscience to help him or her.

The sisters care for forty-nine thousand lepers. They are among the most unwanted, unloved, and neglected people. The other day one of our sisters was washing a leper covered with sores. A Muslim holy man was present, standing close to her. He said, "All these years I have believed that Jesus Christ is a prophet. Today I believe that Jesus Christ is God since he has been able to give such joy to this sister, so that she can do her work with so much love."

The fullness of our heart is expressed in our eyes, in our touch, in what we write, in what we say, in the way we walk, the way we receive, the way we serve. That is the fullness of our heart expressing itself in many different ways.

Charity for the poor is like a living flame; the drier the fuel, the brighter it burns. In your service to the poor do not give only your hands but also your hearts. Charity to be fruitful must cost us. Give until it hurts. To love, it is necessary to give: to give it is necessary to be free from selfishness.

If our poor die of hunger, it is not because God does not care for them. Rather, it is because neither you nor I are generous enough. It is because we are not instruments of love in the hands of God. We do not recognize Christ when once again he appears to us in the hungry man, in the lonely woman, in the child who is looking for a place to get warm.

Try not to judge people. If you judge others then you are not giv-ing love. Instead, try to help them by seeing their needs and acting to meet them. It isn't what anyone may or may not have done, but what you have done that matters in God's eyes.

We must cultivate that sacred silence which makes people remember the words of Jesus: See how they love one another. How often we find ourselves speaking of the faults of another. How often our conversation is about someone who is not pres-ent. Yet see the compassion of Christ toward Judas, the man who received so much love yet betrayed his own master. But the mas-ter kept the sacred silence and did not betray Judas. Jesus could have easily spoken in public—as we often do—telling the hidden intentions and deeds of Judas to others. But he didn't. Instead, he showed mercy and charity. Rather than condemning Judas, he called him his friend.

At times, I feel rather sad, because we do so little. Most people praise us for our actions, but what we do is not more than a drop of water in the ocean. It hardly affects the immensity of human suffering.

One thing that I ask of you: Never be afraid of giving. There is a deep joy in giving, since what we receive is much more than what we give.

The Poor and Poverty

I choose the poverty of our poor people. But I am grateful to receive it (the Nobel) in the name of the hungry, the naked, the homeless, of the crippled, of the blind, of the lepers, of all those people who feel unwanted, unloved, uncared for throughout society, people that have become a burden to the society and are shunned by everyone.

—Mother Teresa accepting the Nobel Peace Prize,
October 17, 1979

The poor give us much more than we give them. They're such strong people, living day to day with no food. And they never curse, never complain. We don't have to give them pity or sympathy. We have so much to learn from them.

When I pick up a hungry person from the street, I give him a plate of rice, a piece of bread. But a person who is shut out, who feels unwanted, unloved, terrified, the person who has been thrown out of society—that spiritual poverty is much harder to overcome.

All my years of service to the poor have helped me to understand that they are precisely the ones who better understand human dignity. If they have a problem, it is not lack of money, but the fact that their right to be treated humanly and with tenderness is not recognized.

Whoever the poorest of the poor are, they are Christ for us—Christ under the guise of human suffering.

To know the problem of poverty intellectually is not to understand it. It is not by reading, taking a walk in the slums, admiring and regretting, that we come to understand it and to discover what it has of bad and good. We have to dive into it, live it, share it.

❧

Today it is very fashionable to talk about the poor. Unfortunately, it is not fashionable to talk with them.

❧

I once picked up a small girl who was wandering the streets, lost. Hunger was written all over her face. Who knows how long it had been since she had eaten anything! I offered her a piece of bread. The little one started eating, crumb by crumb. I told her, "Eat, eat the bread! Aren't you hungry?" She looked at me and said, "I am just afraid that when I run out of bread, I'll still be hungry."

In many places, children are neglected, but animals are cared for and pampered. Animals are given special food and special things. I love dogs myself very much, but still I cannot bear seeing a dog given the place of a child.

I believe that people today think the poor are not humans like them. They look down on them. But if they had a deep respect for the poor, I am sure it would be easy for them to come closer to them, and to see that they have as much right to the things of life and to love as anybody has.

And today, it is the same Christ, the same Jesus, the same today in our poor people, who are unwanted, unemployed, uncared for, hungry and naked and homeless. They are useless to the state or to society, and nobody has time for them. And it is you and I as Christians who, worthy of that love of Christ, if our love is true, must find them. We must help them, they are there for the finding.

Before God we are all poor. We are all handicapped in one way or another. Sometimes it can be seen on the outside, sometimes it is in the inside. The healthy person may be closer to dying or even more dead than the person who is dying. They might be spiritually dead, only it does not show.

Poverty doesn't only consist of being hungry for bread, but rather it is a tremendous hunger for human dignity. We need to love and to be somebody for someone else. This is where we make our mistake and shove people aside. Not only have we denied the poor a piece of bread, but by thinking that they have no worth and leaving them abandoned in the streets, we have denied them the human dignity that is rightfully theirs as children of God.

Abandonment is an awful poverty. There are poor people everywhere, but the deepest poverty is not being loved.

But in the West you have another kind of poverty, spiritual poverty. This is far worse. People do not believe in God, do not pray. People do not care for each other. You have the poverty of people who are dissatisfied with what they have, who do not know how to suffer, who give in to despair. This poverty of heart is often more difficult to relieve and to defeat.

Our constitutions state: "We and our poor will rely entirely on divine providence. We are not ashamed to beg from door to door as members of Christ, who himself lived on alms during the public life and whom we serve in the sick and the poor."

Poverty makes us free. We need to experience the joy of poverty. We choose poverty, we choose not to have things, unlike the poorest of the poor who are forced to be poor. If we do not have something, it is because we choose not to have it. In this, we are free because nothing belongs to us. Our poverty means that we do not have the kind of shoes we may want or the house we may want. We cannot keep things or give anything away or lend anything of value. We have nothing. We own nothing. This is the experience of poverty.

How can you truly know the poor unless you live like them? If they complain about the food, we can say that we eat the same. The more we have the less we can give. Poverty is a wonderful gift because it gives us freedom—it means we have fewer obstacles to God.

Some people would advise me to change certain things. For instance, they tell me that the sisters should have fans in the common room or in the chapel. I do not want them to have fans. The poor whom they are to serve have no fans. Most of the girls come from village homes where they had no fans. They should not be more comfortable here than at home. The same is true for the routine of the house. I always ask these people, "Please do not interfere!"

Rigorous poverty is our safeguard. We do not want, as has been the case with other religious orders throughout history, to begin serving the poor and then gradually move toward serving the rich. In order for us to understand and to be able to help those who lack everything, we have to live as they live. The difference lies only in the fact that those we aid are poor by force, whereas we are poor by choice.

Family Life

I cannot forget my mother. She was usually very busy all day long. But when sunset drew near, it was her custom to hurry with her tasks in order to be ready to receive my father. At the time we did not understand, and we would smile and even joke a little about it. Today I cannot help but call to mind that great delicacy of love that she had for him. No matter what happened, she was always prepared, with a smile on her lips, to welcome him.

To parents: It is very important that children learn from their fathers and mothers how to love one another—not in the school, not from the teacher, but from you. It is very important that you share with your children the joy of that smile. There will be misunderstandings; every family has its cross, its suffering. Always be the first to forgive with a smile. Be cheerful, be happy.

Try to put in the hearts of your children a love for home. Make them long to be with their families. So much sin could be avoided if our people really loved their homes.

Everybody today seems to be in such a terrible rush, anxious for greater development and greater riches, so that children have very little time for their parents. And parents have very little time for their children and for each other. So the breakdown of peace in the world begins at home.

It is easy to smile at people outside your own home. It is so easy to take care of the people that you don't know well. It is difficult to be thoughtful and kind and to smile and be loving to your own in the house day after day, especially when we are tired and in a bad temper or bad mood. We all have these moments and that is the time that Christ comes to us in a distressing disguise.

Sometimes people can hunger for more than bread. It is possible that our children, our husband, our wife, do not hunger for bread, do not need clothes, do not lack a house. But are we equally sure that none of them feels alone, abandoned, neglected, needing some affection? That, too, is poverty.

Bring love into your homes. If you truly love God, start loving your son or your daughter and your spouse. And the elderly, where are they? In nursing homes! Why are they not with you? And where is the retarded child? In an institution! Why is he not with you? That child, young mothers and fathers, is a gift from God.

Bring prayer back into your family life, and you too will see that unity, the bond of joyful love that will bind you together. Maybe there is poverty and suffering in your families. But sharing together, loving together will help you.

St. Joseph knew, when Mary became pregnant, that this child was not his child. He saw that she was pregnant but didn't know how. If he had gone to the high priest, she would have been stoned to death. Do you see the charity and thoughtfulness of St. Joseph? If we have that same kind of charity and thoughtfulness toward each other, our families will become the abode of the Most High. How beautiful our families will become where there is total thoughtfulness for others.

We are commanded to love God and our neighbor equally, without difference. We don't have to look for the opportunities to fill this command, they're all around us, twenty-four hours a day. You must open your eyes wide so that you can see the opportunities to give wholehearted, free service right where you are, in your family. If you don't give such service in your family, you will not be able to give it to those outside your home.

Peace in the World

Please choose the way of peace. . . . In the short term there may be winners and losers in this war that we all dread. But that never can, nor never will justify the suffering, pain, and loss of life your weapons will cause.

—Letter to George H. W. Bush and Saddam Hussein,
January 1991

Let us not use bombs and guns to overcome the world. Let us use love and compassion. Peace begins with a smile. Smile five times a day at someone you don't really want to smile at all. Do it for peace. Let us radiate the peace of God and so light his light and extinguish in the world and in the hearts of all men all hatred and love for power.

Whereas you work to bring about peace, why is it you do not work, they ask, to lessen war? If you are working for peace, that peace lessens war. But I won't mix in politics. War is the fruit of politics, and so I don't involve myself, that's all. If I get stuck in politics, I will stop loving. Because I will have to stand by one, and not by all. This is the difference.

Every act of love is a work of peace, no matter how small.

If peace and love are not allowed to take their rightful place at the table of negotiation, then hatred and anger will produce a conflict that will continue for many years to come. It will solve nothing and thousands of innocent lives will be lost. I ask you all to pray for peace which is such an urgent priority.

I have never been in a war before, but I have seen famine and death. I was asking (myself) what do they feel when they do this? I don't understand it. They are all children of God.

All of us must intend to work in a special way for the sake of peace. In order to bring about that peace, all of us must learn from Jesus to be meek and humble of heart. Only humility will lead us to unity, and unity to peace.

The Holy Father spoke in one of his messages about peace, and one thing he said was this: "No to violence and yes to peace." What is violence? In the first place, we think of weapons, knives, killings. We never think of connecting violence with our tongues. But the first weapon, the most cruel weapon, is the tongue. Examine what part your tongue has played in creating peace or violence. We can really wound a person, we can kill a person, with our tongue.

I feel that we too often focus on the negative aspects of life, on what is bad. If we were more willing to see the good and the beautiful things that surround us, we would be able to transform our families. From there, we would change our next-door neighbors and then others who live in our neighborhood or city. We would be able to bring peace and love to our world, which hungers so much for these things.

We must live life beautifully; we have Jesus with us and he loves us. If we could only remember that God loves us, and we have an opportunity to love others as he loves us, not in big things, but in small things with great love, then [our country] becomes a nest of love . . . a burning light of peace in the world.

Speaking to Youth

As the new graduates go out, I thought that the prayer of Cardinal Newman is most fitting for them, so that, in going into the world, they go with Jesus, they work for Jesus, and serve him in the distressing guise of the poor. Dear Jesus, help us to spread your fragrance everywhere we go. Flood our souls with your spirit and life. Penetrate and possess our whole being so utterly that all our lives may only be a radiance of yours. Shine through us and be so in us that every person we should come in contact with may feel your presence in our soul. Let them look up and see no longer us, but only Jesus.

—From Mother Teresa's Commencement address
at Harvard University, 1982

We must know that we have been created for greater things, not just to be a number in the world, not just to go for diplomas and degrees, this work and that work. We have been created in order to love and to be loved.

To students: I pray that all those young people who have graduated, do not carry just a piece of paper with them but that they carry with them love, peace, and joy. That they become the sunshine of God's love to our people, the hope of eternal happiness, and the burning flame of love wherever they go. That they become carriers of God's love. That they be able to give what they have received. For they have received not to keep but to share.

Young people, open your hearts to the love of God. He loves you with tenderness, and he will give you not just to give but to share. And the less you have, the more you can give; and the more you have, the less you can give. And so, when you are praying ask, ask for courage, and give and give until it hurts. This kind of giving is love in action.

I am convinced that today's youth are more generous than those of times past. Our youth are better prepared and more willing to sacrifice for the service of man. For that reason, it is no surprise that young people have a preference for our congregation. To a large extent these are young people from the middle class. They have everything: wealth, comfort, high status. However, they ask to enter a congregation that is at the service of the poor, in order to lead a life of real poverty and contemplation.

When, at the very beginning after leaving my convent at Loreto, I arrived in Creek Lane, Calcutta, alone, I had only a box and five rupees. A man from Air India wanted to give me a nice suitcase to carry the few things I had with me. I said to him, "There is no shame in carrying a cardboard box." So also, there is no shame in asking when we need guidance or help. Is it not better for me to ask, than from pride and ignorance to do what is wrong?

You are the future of family life. You are the future of the joy of loving. You are the future of making your life something beautiful for God. . . . That you love a girl or that you love a boy is beautiful, but don't spoil it, don't destroy it. Keep it pure. Keep your heart virgin. Keep your love virgin, so that on the day of your marriage you can give something beautiful to each other . . . the joy of a pure love.

Young people, make a strong resolution today, that we will keep our purity pure, our chastity chaste, our virginity virgin! The greatest gift you can give to each other on the day of your wedding, or to God, on the day when you join the priesthood or religious life, is a pure heart, a pure body.

You young people, full of love and strength, do not waste your energy on useless things. Look and see your brother and your sister, not only here in the United States, not only in your city or your area. Everywhere there are human beings who are hungry and who look to you. There are naked human beings who look hopefully to you. There are dispossessed people who look to you. Do not turn your back on the poor because the poor are Christ.

Prayer, Faith, and Holiness

The fruit of Silence is Prayer.
The fruit of Prayer is Faith.
The fruit of Faith is Love.
The fruit of Love is Service.
The fruit of Service is Peace.

—Message printed on little cards given out by Mother Teresa,
which she referred to as her "business cards"

My secret is very simple: I pray. Through prayer I become one in love with Christ. I realize that praying to him is loving him.

I don't think there is anyone who needs God's help and grace as much as I do. Sometimes I feel so helpless and weak. I think that is why God uses me. Because I cannot depend on my own strength, I rely on him twenty-four hours a day. If the day had even more hours, then I would need his help and grace during those hours as well. All of us must cling to God through prayer.

Prayer is as necessary as the air, as the blood in our bodies, as anything to keep us alive—to keep us alive to the grace of God.

We shall not waste our time in looking for extraordinary experiences in our life of prayer but live by pure faith, ever watchful and ready for his coming by doing our day-to-day ordinary duties with extraordinary love and devotion.

Prayer is not asking. Prayer is putting oneself in the hands of God, at his disposition, and listening to his voice in the depths of our hearts.

We must improve our prayer and, flowing from that, our charity toward others. It can be difficult to pray when we don't know how, but we can help ourselves through the use of silence. Souls of prayer are souls of great silence. This silence takes a lot of sacrifice, but if we really want to pray, we must be ready to take that step now. Without this first step toward silence, we will not be able to reach our goal, which is union with God.

Be faithful to the time spent in prayer and make sure that at least half of your prayer is spent in silence. This will bring you closer to Jesus. If you deepen your prayer life you will grow in holiness and obtain many graces for the souls entrusted to your care. Deepen your love for one another by praying for each other and by sharing thoughts and graces you have received in prayer and reading.

I always begin my prayer in silence, for it is in the silence of the heart that God speaks. God is the friend of silence—we need to listen to God because it's not what we say but what he says to us and through us that matters.

We too are called to withdraw at certain intervals into deeper silence and aloneness with God, together as a community as well as personally. To be alone with him—not with our books, thoughts, and memories but completely stripped of everything— to dwell lovingly in his presence, silent, empty, expectant, and motionless. We cannot find God in noise or agitation.

Love to pray. Take the trouble to pray. Prayer opens your heart until it is big enough to hold and keep God. We must know Jesus in prayer before we can see him in the broken bodies of the poor.

You can pray while you work. Work doesn't stop prayer and prayer doesn't stop work. It requires only that small raising of the mind to him: I love you God, I trust you, I believe in you, I need you now. Small things like that. They are wonderful prayers.

To me, contemplation is not to be shut up in a dark place but to allow Jesus to live his passion, love, and humility in us, praying with us, being with us, sanctifying through us.

Do not have long discussions on prayer. Learn from Jesus how to pray and allow him to pray in you and through you. Then put the fruit of that prayer into living action by loving one another as Jesus loves you.

Everything starts from prayer. Without asking God for love, we cannot possess love and still less are we able to give it to others. Just as people today are speaking so much about the poor but they do not know or talk to the poor, we too cannot talk so much about prayer and yet not know how to pray.

When you first come to know Jesus, you learn how to pray. When you pray, stand straight. When you pray, your vocation is strong. When you pray, you begin to love. When your prayer diminishes, your vocation is in great danger.

Every moment of prayer, especially before our Lord in the tabernacle, is a sure, positive gain. The time we spend in having our daily audience with God is the most precious part of the whole day.

When I was crossing into Gaza, I was asked at the checkpost whether I was carrying any weapons. I replied: Oh yes, my prayer books.

I take the Lord at his word. Faith is a gift of God. Without it there would be no life. And our work, to be fruitful and beautiful, has to be built on faith. Love and faith go together. They complete each other.

Living a Christian life provides for the growth of faith. There have been many saints who have gone before to guide us, but I like the ones who are simple, like St. Thérèse of Lisieux, the Little Flower of Jesus. I chose her as my namesake because she did ordinary things with extraordinary love.

Faith in action is service. We try to be holy because we believe. In most modern rooms you see an electrical light that can be turned on by a switch. But, if there is no connection with the main powerhouse, then there can be no light. Faith and prayer is the connection with God, and when that is there, there is service.

No one can take my faith from me. If, in order to spread the love of Christ among the poor and neglected, there were no alternative but to remain in that country, I would remain—but I would not renounce my faith. I am prepared to give up my life but never my faith.

God does not demand that I be successful. God demands that I be faithful. When facing God, results are not important. Faithfulness is what is important.

Holiness grows fast where there is kindness. I have never heard of kind souls going astray. The world is lost for want of sweetness and kindness.

Nothing can make me holy except the presence of God and to me the presence of God is fidelity to small things. Fidelity to small things will lead you to Christ. Infidelity to small things will lead you to sin.

You have to be holy where you are—wherever God has put you.

I must give myself completely to him. I must not attempt to control God's actions. I must not desire a clear perception of my advance along the road, nor know precisely where I am on the way of holiness. I ask him to make a saint of me, yet I must leave to him the choice of that saintliness itself and still more the choice of the means that lead to it.

Holiness is not something extraordinary, not something for only a few with brains, with intellectual powers that can reason, that can discuss, that can have long talks and read very wonderful books. Holiness is for every one of us as a simple duty—the acceptance of God with a smile, at all times, anywhere and everywhere.

Holiness is not the luxury of the few; it is a simple duty, for you and for me. We have been created for that. So let us be holy as Our Father in Heaven is holy.

Humility

I don't claim anything of the work. It's his work. I'm like a little pencil in his hand. That's all. He does the thinking. He does the writing. The pencil has nothing to do with it. The pencil has only to be allowed to be used.

—From *Time* magazine interview, 1989

If you are humble, nothing will touch you, neither praise nor disgrace, because you know what you are. If you are blamed, you won't be discouraged; if anyone calls you a saint, you won't put yourself on a pedestal.

Humility always radiates the glory and greatness of God. How wonderful are the ways of God who used humility, smallness, helplessness, and poverty to prove his love to the world. Do not be afraid to be humble, small, and helpless in order to prove your love for God.

Let us beg from Our Lady to make our hearts "meek and humble" like her Son's was. We learn humility through accepting humiliations cheerfully. Do not let a chance pass you by. It is so easy to be proud, harsh, moody, and selfish, but we have been created for greater things. Why stoop down to things that will spoil the beauty of our hearts?

A rich man came to Shishu Bhavan (the house of unwanted babies) and said he would give whatever the sisters would ask. He wanted to give a generator. This costs thousands. I told him "no." Today a generator, tomorrow a washing machine. He said, "Mother, all these years I have been producing all kinds of things to make more and more money, but from the time I came into contact with the poor, I want to give." So he gave us some kerosene lamps. We must be convinced of the freedom of our poverty and keep to the most humble of means.

Take away your eyes from yourself and rejoice that you have nothing—that you are nothing—that you can do nothing. Give Jesus a big smile each time your nothingness frightens you. Just keep the joy of Jesus as your strength—be happy and at peace, accept whatever he takes with a big smile.

One cannot expect to become a saint without paying the price, and the price is much renunciation, much temptation, much struggle and persecution, and all sorts of sacrifices. One cannot love God except at the cost of oneself.

I am but an instrument. The first time I received an award, I was very surprised. I did not know whether to accept it or not. But I came to the conclusion that I should accept awards in the name of the poorest poor, as a form of homage to them. I think that basically, when awards are given to me, the existence of the poor in the world is being recognized.

I can't bear being photographed but I make use of everything for the glory of God. When I allow a person to take a photograph, I tell Jesus to take one soul to Heaven out of Purgatory.

Each one of us is merely a small instrument; all of us, after accomplishing our mission, will disappear.

If you are really humble, if you realize how small you are and how much you need God, then you cannot fail.

I am often asked, after Mother Teresa who? That will be no trouble. God will find a more humble person, more obedient to him, more faithful, someone smaller with a deeper faith, and he will do still greater things through her.

Chastity

Chastity touches God himself, it is undivided love for God alone. Nothing and nobody can draw us away from him.

Chastity is not only our ability to give, but more, our ability to accept God's gift. Is it your desire to follow Christ perfectly? Are you resolved to live in chastity? Chastity is a sign of the kingdom of Heaven.

Purity, chastity, and virginity created a special beauty in Mary that attracted God's attention. He showed his great love for the world by giving Jesus to her.

We must be convinced that nothing adorns a human soul with greater splendor than the virtue of chastity and nothing defiles a human soul more than the opposite vice. Yet the glory of chastity is not in immunity from temptation—it is in victory over temptations. A chaste person is not free from temptations but overcomes them.

By my vow of chastity, I not only renounce the married state of life, but I also consecrate to God the free use of my internal and external acts, my affections. I cannot in conscience love another with the love of a woman for a man. I no longer have the right to give that affection to any other creature but only to God.

By our vow of chastity we do renounce God's natural gift to women to become mothers—for the greater gift—that of being virgins for Christ, of entering into a much more beautiful motherhood.

People in the world think that the vow of chastity makes us inhuman, makes us become like stones, without feelings. Each one of us can tell them it is not true. It is the vow of chastity that gives us the freedom to love everybody instead of simply becoming a mother to three or four children. A married woman can love but one man; we can love the whole world in God.

Chastity does not simply mean that we are not married. It means that we love Christ with an undivided love. To be pure we need poverty. Is it wrong to have things? We vow poverty not because it is wrong to have things but we choose to do without these things.

To be able to understand chastity we must know what poverty and obedience are. They are like the pillars. If we remove the pillars, the whole building will tip to one side and fall.

The poor are very great people. They can teach us so many beautiful things. Once one of them came to thank us for teaching her natural family planning and said: "You people who have practiced chastity, you are the best people to teach us natural family planning because it is nothing more than self-control out of love for each other." And what this poor person said is very true.

If you have failed to be chaste, confess it now and be finished with it. God's mercy is greater than your sin. Don't be afraid, scrupulous, or anxious. You are a sinner full of sin when you go to confession, and when you come out, you are a sinner without sin.

Joy

Serve God joyfully. Let there be no sadness in your life: the only true sorrow is sin.

A joyful heart is the normal result of a heart burning with love. Joy is not simply a matter of temperament, it is always hard to remain joyful—all the more reason why we should try to acquire it and make it grow in our hearts.

Joy is prayer; joy is strength, joy is love. God loves a cheerful giver. The best way we can show our gratitude to God and the people is to accept everything with joy.

When you go out for your task, spread all around you the joy of belonging to God, of living with God, of being his own.

If you are joyful, it will shine in your eyes and in your look, in your conversation and in your countenance. You will not be able to hide it because joy overflows.

Joy must be one of the pivots of our life. It is the token of a generous personality. Sometimes it is also a mantle that clothes a life of sacrifice and self-giving. A person who has this gift often reaches high summits. He or she is like a sun in a community.

Let us keep the joy of loving Jesus in our hearts. And let us share that joy with everyone we meet. Passing on joy is something which is very natural. We have no reason for not being joyful, since Christ is with us. Christ is in our hearts. Christ is in the poor we meet. Christ is in the smile we give to others, and he is in the smile we receive from others.

Resist anything that leads to moodiness. Our prayer each day should be, "Let the joy of the Lord be my strength." Cheerfulness and joy were Our Lady's strength. This made her a willing handmaid of God. Only joy could have given her the strength to go in haste over the hills of Judea to her cousin Elizabeth, there to do the work of a handmaid. If we are to be true handmaids of the Lord, then we too, each day, must go cheerfully in haste over the hills of difficulties.

Joy is one of the best safeguards against temptation. The devil is a carrier of dust and dirt and he uses every opportunity to throw what he has at us. But a joyful heart protects us from this dirt. That is because Jesus is there in our joy. Jesus takes full possession of our soul when we surrender to him joyfully.

The joy of the risen Lord is the sunshine of our Father's love. The joy of Jesus is the hope of eternal happiness. The joy of Jesus is the flame of burning love. Easter is this joy. However, you cannot have joy without sacrifice. That is why Good Friday comes before Easter.

Joy comes to those who in a sense forget themselves and become totally aware of the other.

Joy is very infectious. We will never know just how much good a simple smile can do. Be faithful in little things. Smile at one another. We must live beautifully.

The Blessed Mother

Loving trust and total surrender made Our Lady say "yes" to the message of the angel. And cheerfulness made her run in haste to serve her cousin Elizabeth. That is so much our life: saying "yes" to Jesus and running in haste to serve him in the poorest of the poor. Let us keep very close to Our Lady and she will make that same spirit grow in each one of us.

—From Mother Teresa's final letter written
on the day of her death

Let us ask Our Lady to keep us company, to stay with us. Let us ask Mary, who besides being the Mother of Jesus, is so beautiful, so pure, so immaculate, and full of grace! If Mary stays with us, we can keep Jesus in our hearts, so that we can love and serve him through ministry to the poorest of the poor.

Mary showed complete trust in God by agreeing to be used as an instrument in his plan of salvation. She trusted him in spite of her nothingness because she knew he who is mighty could do great things in her and through her. Once she said "yes" to him, she never doubted. She was just a young woman, but she belonged to God and nothing nor anyone could separate her from him.

When the fullness of grace became one with the Word of God in her, the fruit of that union was Mary's service of love to her neighbor. She didn't dwell on the Son of God within her or on the joy and sorrow that were to be hers as the Mother of God and men.

The vocation of Our Lady was to accept Jesus into her life. She accepted being the handmaid of the Lord. Then, in haste, she went to give Jesus to St. John the Baptist and his mother. Today the same living Jesus comes to us and we too, like Mary, must go in haste to give him to others.

Mary did not feel ashamed. She proclaimed Jesus her son. At Calvary we see her standing upright—the mother of God, standing next to the cross. What a deep faith she must have had because of her love for her son! To see him dishonored, unloved, an object of hatred. Yet, she stayed upright.

Pray especially to Our Blessed Mother Mary, placing all your intentions into her hands. For she loves you as she loves her Son. She will guide you in all your relationships so that peace may fill your life.

A gentleman of the Protestant faith, the son-in-law of Malcolm Muggeridge, told me: "I love you, your work, everything I see, but there is one thing I do not understand: Our Lady. You are full of Mary." I replied to him: "No Mary, no Jesus—no mother, no son."

A few months later he sent me a card with these words printed in big letters: "I believe, no Mary, no Jesus! This has changed my life."

We have a mother in Heaven, the Virgin Mary, who is a guide for us, a great joy, and an important source of our cheerfulness in Christ. Intercede with her before God. Pray the Rosary so that Mary may always be with you, to be your guide, to protect and keep you as a mother. Introduce prayer into your families. The family that prays together, stays together.

Let us ask Our Lady, in a very special way: Mary, mother of Jesus, be a mother to each of us, that we, like you, may be pure in heart, that we, like you, love Jesus; that we, like you, serve the poorest for we are all poor. First let us love our neighbors and so fulfill God's desire that we become carriers of his love and compassion.

Mary is our mother, the cause of our joy. Being a mother, I have never had difficulty in talking with Mary and feeling close to her.

The Gift of Life

We are here to be witnesses of love and to celebrate life, because life has been created in the image of God. Life is to love and to be loved. That is why we all have to take a strong stand so that no child—boy or girl—will be rejected or unloved. Every child is a sign of God's love, that has to be extended over all the earth.

Each one of us is here today because we have been loved by God who created us and our parents who accepted and cared enough to give us life. Life is the most beautiful gift of God. That is why it is so painful to see what is happening today in so many places around the world; life being deliberately destroyed by war, by violence, by abortion.

A great poverty reigns in a country that allows taking the life of an unborn child—a child created in God's image, created to live and to love. His or her life is not for destroying but for living, despite the selfishness of those who fear that they lack the means to feed or educate one more child.

If a mother can kill her own child, how long will it be before we start to kill one another? We should not be surprised when we hear about murders, deaths, wars, and hate in the world today. Don't ever allow even one child, born or unborn, to be unwanted. Let us go with Our Lady to search out that child and take him or her home.

A Hindu woman told me: "I had an abortion eight years ago. Until today, every time I see a child eight years old, I turn my head. I can't look at that child. Every year, when I see a child six, seven years old, I say, "Oh, my child would have been seven years old, he could be holding my hand."

Why does she say this? Because it is impossible to break the gift of God within us, the love that he has created in us.

If you hear of someone who does not want to have her child, who wants to have an abortion, try to convince her to bring the child to me. I will love that child, who is a sign of God's love. . . . I don't think any human heart should dare to take life, or any human hand be raised to destroy life. Life is the life of God in us. Life is the greatest gift that God has bestowed on human beings, and man has been created in the image of God. Life belongs to God, and we have no right to destroy it.

People very often make jokes with me (or about me, rather), because we are also teaching natural family planning. They say, "Mother Teresa is doing plenty of talking about family planning, but she herself does not practice it. She is having more and more children every day."

I can never forget the time when I gave a child to a family and after a few months I heard that the child had become very, very sick. I went to the family and told them: "Give me back that child. I'll take care of the sick child and I'll give you another healthy child." The father looked at me and said, "Mother, take my life rather than the child."

It is true, people are very anxious about the future and about over-population. But there is natural family planning. That method can help couples plan their family without destroying God's gift of life. . . . By properly using the natural family planning method, couples are using their bodies to glorify God in the sanctity of family life. I think that if we could bring this method to every country, if our poor people would learn it, there would be more peace, more love in the family between parents and children.

Abortion destroys the image of God. It is the most terrible plague in our society, the greatest killer of love and peace. Those little children still unborn have been created for bigger things: to love and to be loved.

Suffering and Death

There is much suffering in the world—physical, material, mental. The suffering of some can be blamed on the greed of others. The material and physical suffering is suffering from hunger, from homelessness, from all kinds of diseases. But the greatest suffering is being lonely, feeling unloved, having no one. I have come more and more to realize that it is being unwanted that is the worst disease that any human being can ever experience.

When suffering overtakes us, let us accept it with a smile. This is the greatest gift of God: having the courage to accept with a smile whatever he gives us and whatever he takes from us.

If you accept suffering and offer it to God, that gives you joy. Suffering is a great gift of God; those who accept it willingly, those who love deeply, those who offer themselves know its value.

❧

Sacrifice, surrender, and suffering are not popular topics nowadays. Our culture makes us believe that we can have it all, that we should demand our rights, that with the right technology all pain and problems can be overcome. That is not my attitude toward sacrifice.

❧

Remember that the passion of Christ ends always in the joy of the resurrection of Christ, so when you feel in your own heart the suffering of Christ, remember the resurrection has to come. Never let anything so fill you with sorrow as to make you forget the joy of Christ risen.

My thoughts often run to you who suffer, and I offer your sufferings, which are so great, while mine are so small. Those of you who are sick, when things are hard, take refuge in Christ's heart. There my own heart will find with you strength and love.

Some remind me of what a magazine once said about me; it described me as a "living saint." If someone sees God in me, I am happy. I see God in everyone, and especially in those who suffer.

In my heart, I carry the last glances of the dying. I do all I can so that they feel loved at that most important moment when a seemingly useless existence can be redeemed.

Every day is a preparation for death. By realizing this, it helps somehow, because what the dying go through today, I will go through tomorrow. Death is nothing except going back to him, where he is and where we belong.

Death is the most decisive moment in human life. It is like our coronation: to die in peace with God.

If you were to die today, what would others say about you? What was in you that was beautiful, that was Christlike, that helped others to pray better? Face yourself, with Jesus at your side, and do not be satisfied with just any answer.

One day, however, we will have to meet the Lord of the universe. What will we tell him about that child, about that old father or mother? They are his creatures, children of God. What will be our answer?

I remember that at the beginning of my work I had a very high fever and in that delirious fever I went before Saint Peter. He said to me, "Go back! There are no slums in Heaven!" So I got very angry with him and I said, "Very well! Then, I will fill Heaven with slum people and you will have slums then!" When somebody dies, that person has gone home to God. That's where we all have to go.

People die suddenly all the time, so it could happen to us too at any moment. Yesterday is gone and tomorrow has not yet come; we must live each day as if it were our last so that when God calls us we are ready, and prepared, to die with a clean heart.

Sin and Forgiveness

When we realize that we are all sinners needing forgiveness, it will be easy for us to forgive others. We have to be forgiven in order to be able to forgive. If I do not understand this, it will be very hard for me to say, "I forgive you" to anyone who comes to me.

If you feel the weight of your sins, do not be afraid! He is a loving Father; God's mercy is much greater than we can imagine.

Violence of the tongue is very real—sharper than any knife, wounding and creating bitterness that only the grace of God can heal.

Never stop to do anything secretly. Hiding is the beginning of lying, lie in action.

If we deliberately allow venial sin to become a daily bread, a moral anemia, the soul becomes weak all around, the spiritual life begins to crumble and fall apart. God preserve us from any deliberate sin, no matter how small it may be. Nothing is small when it means going against God.

My sister and I used to read the same books. One day my sister read a book and passed it to me. As soon as I read two pages, I felt it would be a sin to read that book. Later I asked my sister whether she had read the book. She replied that she had and had found nothing wrong in it. There was no sin in my sister reading the book, but in conscience I could not read it.

Every human being comes from the hand of God, and we all know something of God's love for us. Whatever our religion, we know that if we really want to love, we must first learn to forgive before anything else.

Forgive and ask to be forgiven; excuse rather than accuse.

Penance calls us away from sin and to God. It leads us away from mediocrity and to a life of fervor, generosity, and sanctity.

When someone is doing something to hurt you, don't turn inward, turn toward that person. He is hurting himself. You must learn to forgive, knowing that we all need forgiveness. If you want to be true to God, you must learn from Jesus to be meek, humble, and pure.

Let us be very sincere in our dealings with each other and have the courage to accept each other as we are. Do not be surprised at or become preoccupied with each other's failure; rather see and find the good in each other, for each one of us is created in the image of God.

Money

Money? I never give it a thought. It always comes. We do all our work for our Lord; he must look after us. If he wants something to be done, he must give us the means. If he does not provide us with the means, then it shows that he does not want that particular work. I forget about it.

Riches, both material and spiritual, can choke you if you do not use them fairly. For not even God can put anything in a heart that is already full. One day there springs up the desire for money and for all that money can provide—the superfluous, luxury in eating, luxury in dressing, trifles. Needs increase because one thing calls for another. The result is uncontrollable dissatisfaction. Let us remain as empty as possible so that God can fill us up.

Nothing will destroy our joy of loving Jesus as much as money. It is one of the keys of the devil that will open any heart. It is the beginning of great evil.

When one comes in touch with money, one loses contact with God. May God keep us from that; death is to be preferred.

Those who have had many possessions, who have had many goods and riches, are obsessed by them. They think that the only thing that counts is possessing wealth. That is why it is so difficult for them to leave all things. It is much easier for the poor, who are so free, for this freedom allows them to depart with joy.

I think that a person who is attached to riches, who lives with the worry of riches, is actually very poor. If this person puts his money at the service of others, then he is rich, very rich.

Many people think, especially in the West, that having money makes you happy. I think it must be harder to be happy if you are wealthy because you may find it difficult to see God: you'll have too many other things to think about. However, if God has given you this gift of wealth, then use it for his purpose—help others, help the poor, create jobs, give work to others. Don't waste your wealth.

To business people, Lions, Rotarians, Knights and others who come with generous checks: I hope that what you give me comes not from your surplus but it is the fruit of a sacrifice made for the love of God. You must give what costs you, go without something you like, then you will truly be brothers to the poor who are deprived of even the things they need.

Let us not be satisfied just by giving money. Money is not everything. Money is something you can get. The poor need the work of our hands, the love of our hearts. Love, an abundant love, is the expression of our Christian religion.

Who are we to judge the rich? It is our duty to put the poor and the rich face to face, to be their point of encounter.

Religion

To me, to be a Christian is very important. To me it means every-thing, because each individual has to act according to the grace God gives to his soul. God gives to every soul that he has created a chance to come face to face with him, to accept him or to reject him. God has his own ways and means to work in the hearts of men and we do not know how close they are to him. But by their actions we will always know whether they are at his disposal or not. How you live your life is the proof that you are or not fully his, whether one is a Hindu or a Muslim or a Christian.

In order to be Christians, we should resemble Christ, of this I am firmly convinced. Gandhi once said that if Christians lived according to their faith, there would be no more Hindus left in India. People expect us to be consistent with our Christian life.

Often we Christians constitute the worst obstacle for those who try to become closer to Christ; we often preach a gospel we do not live. This is the principle reason why people of the world don't believe.

But, who is the church? You and I. Jesus doesn't need palaces. Only men need them. The church are those who follow him. Following him is something that I try to do every day. We live surrounded by people who are hungry for love. That is what we need to give them.

Some in our country call God Ishwar. Others call him Allah. And others just call him God. Every one of us has to recognize that he created us for greater things, such as to love and be loved. Who are we to keep our people from looking for God who has created them, who loves them, and to whom we all must return one day?

There is only one God and he is God to all; therefore it is important that everyone is seen as equal before God. I've always said we should help a Hindu become a better Hindu, a Muslim become a better Muslim, a Catholic become a better Catholic.

I love all religions but I am in love with my own. If people become better Hindus, better Muslims, better Buddhists by our acts of love, then there is something else growing there. They come closer and closer to God. When they come closer, they have to choose.

Religion is not something that you and I can dictate. Religion is the worship of God, and therefore it is a matter of conscience. Each one of us must decide how we are going to worship. In my case, the religion that I live and practice is Roman Catholicism. It is my life, my joy, and the greatest proof of God's love for me. . . . I cannot force anyone to accept my religion—just as no man, no law, and no government can legally demand that anyone reject a religion that promises them peace, joy, and love.

I believe that God has created each soul, that that soul belongs to God, and that each soul has to find God in its own lifetime and enter into his life. That is what is important. All of us need to seek God and find him.

We never base our assistance on the religious beliefs of the needy but on the need itself. We are not concerned with the religious beliefs of those we help. We only focus on how urgent the need is.

We have absolutely no difficulty regarding having to work in countries with many faiths. We treat all people as children of God. They are our brothers and sisters. We show great respect to them. Our work is to encourage these people, Christians as well as non-Christians, to do works of love. Every work of love done with a full heart brings people closer to God.

Women

To women: You and I, being women, we have this tremendous thing in us, understanding love. I see that so beautifully in our people, in our poor women, who day after day, meet suffering, accept suffering for the sake of their children. I have seen mothers going without so many things, even resorting to begging, so that the children may have what they need.

Every woman can be equal to men if we have brains and if we have money. But no man can become equal to women in love and in ability to show service.

I think this is the wonderful tenderness of a woman's heart: to be aware of the suffering of others and to try to spare them that suffering, as Mary did. Do you and I have that same tenderness in our hearts? Do we have Mary's eyes for discovering the needs of others?

Motherhood is the gift of God to women. How grateful we must be to God for this wonderful gift that brings such joy to the whole world, women and men alike! Yet we can destroy this gift of motherhood, especially by the evil of abortion, but also by thinking that other things like jobs or positions are more important than loving, than giving oneself to others. No job, no plans, no possessions, no idea of "freedom" can take the place of love.

I do not understand why some people are saying that women and men are exactly the same, and are denying the beautiful differences between men and women. All God's gifts are good, but they are not all the same.

What a woman can give, no man can give. That is why God has created them separately. . . . Woman is created to be the heart of the family, the heart of love. If we miss that, we miss everything. They give that love in the family or they give it in service, that is what their creation is for.

Mothers make the home a center of love. Their role is sometimes hard, but there is the example of the Blessed Virgin, who teaches us to be good with our children. We Missionaries of Charity also have to be mothers and make our communities happy homes.

Why did God make some of us men and others women? Because a woman's love is one image of the love of God, and a man's love is another image of God's love. Both are created to love, but each in a different way. Woman and man complete each other, and together show forth God's love more fully than either can do it alone.

God told us, "Love your neighbor as yourself." So first I am to love myself rightly, and then to love my neighbor like that. But how can I love myself unless I accept myself as God has made me? Those who deny the beautiful differences between men and women are not accepting themselves as God has made them, and so cannot love the neighbor. They will only bring division, unhappiness, and destruction of peace to the world.

The woman is the heart of the home. Let us pray that we women realize the reason of our existence: to love and be loved and through this love become instruments of peace in the world.

The Religious Life

To join the congregation we need few things. We need health of mind and body. We need the ability to learn. We need plenty of common sense and a cheerful disposition. I think common sense and cheerfulness are very necessary for a work like this.

The most appealing invitation to embrace the religious life is the witness of our own lives, the spirit in which we react to our divine calling, the completeness of our dedication, the generosity and cheerfulness of our service to God, the love we have for one another, the apostolic zeal with which we witness to Christ's love for the poorest of the poor.

Diligence, eagerness, fervor, is the test of love; and the test of fervor is the willingness to devote one's own life to working for souls. We must not feel attached to a single place; we must be willing to go all over the world.

A Missionary of Charity is a messenger of God's love, a living lamp that offers its light to all, and the salt of the earth. We are to take Christ to those places where he has not yet been taken.

We the Missionaries of Charity carry out an offensive of love, of prayer, of sacrifice on behalf of the poorest poor. We want to conquer the world through love, and thus bring to everyone's heart the love of God and the proof that God loves the world.

Someone once asked me, "Are you married?" And I said, "Yes, and I find it sometimes very difficult to smile at Jesus because he can be very demanding."

Lord, grant that I may always bear in mind the very great dignity of my vocation, and all its responsibilities. Never let me dishonor it by being cold, or unkind, or impatient.

Our lives have to continuously feed on the Eucharist. If we were not able to see Christ under the appearance of bread, neither would it be possible for us to discover him under the humble appearances of the bruised bodies of the poor.

We are entirely at the disposal of the church. We profess a deep, personal love for the Holy Father. We surrender ourselves completely to be united with him as carriers of God's love. Pray for us that we don't spoil the work God has called us to do.

The work that we Missionaries of Charity are doing is only a means to put our love for Christ in a loving, in a living action. It is so beautiful that we complete each other! What we are doing in the slums, maybe you cannot do. What you are doing in the level where you are called—in your family life, in your college life, in your work—we cannot do. But you and we together are doing something beautiful for God.

How is it that nowadays all over the world so many priests and nuns abandon their calling? Were they not chosen by Christ? Did they not commit themselves to follow him after long and mature reflection? How then can a nun pronounce perpetual vows, and some years later give up the religious life? Are married people not bound to remain faithful to each other until death? Then, why should the same rule not apply to priests and nuns?

It is much easier to conquer a country than to conquer ourselves. Every act of disobedience weakens my spiritual life. It is like a wound letting out every drop of one's blood. Nothing can cause this havoc in our spiritual life as quickly as disobedience.

Many congregations have discarded this vow of obedience. They don't have superiors anymore. Each member makes her own decisions. They have discarded obedience completely. Do you know what has happened because of that? In the United States alone fifty thousand nuns have left the religious life. The destruction of religious life comes mainly from the lack of obedience. Sheer negligence destroys religious life completely.

If we can realize that we religious sisters are the slave girls of the Lord, just as the Virgin Mary was, then the future of religious life will be holy. We religious sisters are like the heart of our mother the church.

Offer to God all your words, your actions. We are to be brides of Christ. Let it never be said that there is a woman in this world who loves her husband more than we love Christ.

Never lose the chance to become like Jesus. We profess before the world, "I am the spouse of Jesus crucified." Like the woman at the altar who professes before the world her marriage to one man, we, too, change our name to show that we belong to Jesus completely.

I will pick the roses. The sharper the thorns, the sweeter shall be my song. For the aim of joining is not to become social workers. Our work is not a profession, but a vocation chosen to satisfy the thirst of Jesus by total surrender, without counting the cost.

Offer to God all your words, your actions. We are to be brides of Christ. Let it never be said that there is a woman in this world who loves her husband more than we love Christ.

Remembering Mother Teresa

Mother Teresa marked the history of our century with courage. She served all human beings by promoting their dignity and respect, and made those who had been defeated by life feel the tenderness of God.

—Pope John Paul II

When she walked into the room to greet me, I felt that I was indeed meeting a saint.

—The Reverend Billy Graham

Hers was a ministry of action, of passion, and compassion. She led by serving and showed us the stunning power of simple humility. Her unconquerable faith touched the lives of millions of people in India, here in the United States, and all around the world.

—Bill Clinton, 42nd U.S. President

This evening, there is less love, less compassion, less light in the world. She leaves us a strong message, which has no borders and which goes beyond faith: helping, listening, solidarity.

—Jacques Chirac, French President

She is the United Nations. She is peace in the world.

—Javier Perez de Cuellar,
former U.N. Secretary-General

Words fail me to express my sorrow at the demise of the apostle of peace and love. . . . Mother Teresa is no more with us. The world and especially India is poorer by her passing away. Her life was devoted to bringing love, peace and joy to people whom the world generally shuns.

—Inder Kumar Gujral,
former Indian Prime Minister

The humanity of the world has lost its Mother. I consider the loss not only irreparable for the country but for the whole world.

—Sitaram Kesri, former leader of
India's Congress Party

We have lost a great soul. She did a great service to humanity. She will be remembered in India and abroad as a person who treated members of various faiths as equal and served them with dedication and devotion.

—K. L. Sharma, spokesman for the
Bharatiya Janata Party of India

Mother Teresa personified a boldness of spirit and purity of soul revered by the entire world. . . . She served as a model of holiness, virtue, and humility.

—Ronald Reagan and Nancy Reagan,
40th U.S. President and First Lady

Her example reminded us of the inherent goodness found in the quiet corners of the human heart.

—Al Gore, former U.S. Vice President

Mother Teresa was a devoted religious daughter of the Church and an extraordinary missionary with tremendous zeal and energy. The witness of her life has been a model of simplicity, piety, and charity.

—Archbishop Theodore McCarrick,
Archdiocese of Washington

Mother Teresa's life proved that the only real revolution in human affairs flows from service to others and self-sacrifice out of love for Jesus Christ. She was a champion of the unwanted, from the outcast of Calcutta to the unwanted unborn of America. She was the genius of the little way of doing great things. Above all, she was in every sense a woman of the Gospel: strong in forgiving, tender to the poor, in love with Jesus Christ, and a servant of his Church.

—Archbishop Charles J. Chaput,
Archdiocese of Denver

A rare and unique individual who lived long for higher purposes. Her lifelong devotion to the care of the poor, the sick, and the disadvantaged was one of the highest examples of service to humanity.

—Nawaz Sharif,
former Prime Minister of Pakistan

All the life of this great woman was the bright incarnation of service to the high humanitarian ideals of goodness, compassion, selflessness, and faith. Mother Teresa will always remain in the hearts and minds of Russians as a friend of our country, ready to render help at any moment.

—Boris Yeltsin, former Russian President

Mother Teresa of Calcutta was one of the most illuminated figures of the Catholic Church at the end of this century. Humanity has lost its symbol of solidarity.

—Fernando Henrique Cardoso,
former Brazilian President

Mother Teresa was a truly exceptional human being whose deep spirituality and compassion for the world's suffering multitudes was an inspiring example.

—Jean Chrétien,
former Canadian Prime Minister

A loss to the entire humanity. She will be deeply missed in our efforts to build international peace, and a just, caring, and equitable world order.

—Nelson Mandela, former
South African President

Our world has lost the most celebrated saint of our times. This courageous woman gave hope to millions, and showed us the power of caring and human kindness.

—Coretta Scott King, civil rights leader
and widow of Martin Luther King, Jr.

Chronology

August 27, 1910—Agnes Gonxha Bojaxhiu is born in Skopje (what is today Macedonia). The youngest of three children born to Nikolle Bojaxhiu and Drana Bernai, she has one sister and one brother.

September 26, 1928—Having felt a strong calling to the religious life earlier in the year, Agnes is admitted provisionally to the Order of the Sisters of Our Lady of Loreto, an Irish order that does missionary work in India. She travels to the motherhouse of the Sisters of Our Lady of Loreto, in Dublin.

December 1, 1928—Agnes studies English for several months in Dublin, and then sets out for India to begin her novitiate in Darjeeling.

May 1931—Agnes spends two years as a novice and then professes temporary vows with the Sisters of Our Lady of Loreto. She takes the name of Teresa, after St. Thérèse of Lisieux, the patron saint of the missions.

1931–1937—Sister Teresa begins teaching at St. Mary's High School in Calcutta. She later professes her final vows as a Sister of Our Lady of Loreto, and becomes the director of curriculum at St. Mary's. Sister Teresa is dedicated to her work and is very happy teaching at St. Mary's School.

September 10, 1946—Sister Teresa is traveling on a train from Calcutta to Darjeeling when she receives a calling from God to live among and serve the poorest of the poor.

August 1948—Though the decision to leave the Sisters of Loreto is for Sister Teresa the hardest thing she is ever called to do, she is convinced it is God's will for her. She receives permission from Rome to leave the Sisters and to devote herself as a nun living and working among the poor. She dons a simple, white sari with a blue border in homage to the Blessed Mother. She leaves Calcutta to take an intensive nursing course for three months, then returns to Calcutta, ready to begin serving the poorest of the poor.

December 1948—Sister Teresa receives permission to open her first school. It is located in a public park, and she teaches such things as basic hygiene to the children. The children call her Mother Teresa.

March 19, 1949—Mother Teresa receives her first follower. She is one of Mother Teresa's former students who visits and asks to join in her mission.

October 7, 1950—The community that Mother Teresa has founded, the Missionaries of Charity, is recognized by the Vatican. The order begins with twelve members. They take vows of chastity, poverty, obedience, and wholehearted, free service to the poorest of the poor.

1952—The order opens Nirmal Hriday, a home for the dying destitutes, on the Feast of the Immaculate Heart of Mary.

1953—The Missionaries of Charity obtain a motherhouse in Calcutta. The sisters later rent and then buy a home for orphaned children on the same street.

1960—By this year, the Missionaries of Charity have opened twenty-five homes in India.

February 1, 1965—There are approximately 300 sisters in the order. Pope Paul VI authorizes the Missionaries of Charity to expand their work outside of India. The first home is opened outside of India, in Venezuela.

1965–1971—Additional homes are opened around the world, including in Africa, in Australia, and in Europe (Italy and England). Pope Paul VI grants Mother Teresa Vatican citizenship to aid in her missionary travels. By 1971, the order has fifty homes.

1969—The Co-workers of the Missionaries of Charity are approved by Pope Paul VI and officially established. The Co-workers are a worldwide organization of lay men and women who further the goals of the Missionaries of Charity.

1971—The Missionaries of Charity open their first home in the United States, in the South Bronx, New York.

1970s—Mother Teresa receives several international awards including the Good Samaritan Award in the United States, the Templeton Award for Progress in Religion in England, and the Pope John XXIII Peace Prize at the Vatican.

October 17, 1979—Mother Teresa is awarded the Nobel Peace Prize. In December 1979, she accepts the award in the name "of all those people who feel unwanted, unloved, uncared for throughout society."

1980–1985—The Missionaries of Charity open many new homes including homes for drug addicts, prostitutes, and battered women around the world. An AIDS hospice is opened in New York. Mother Teresa is awarded the Medal of Freedom, the highest U.S. civilian award.

1986–1989—The Missionaries of Charity are permitted to open homes in places previously closed to missionaries, including Nicaragua, Cuba, and Russia.

1988—The Missionaries of Charity open a homeless shelter at the Vatican.

1988–1989—Mother Teresa is sent to the hospital twice for heart trouble. She has a pacemaker installed and is ordered by her doctors to rest for six months.

April 16, 1990—Mother Teresa resigns as Superior General of the Missionaries of Charity due to her poor health.

September 1990—Mother Teresa is reelected by a conclave of sisters in a secret ballot and leaves retirement to resume her role as the Superior General of the order.

1993—Mother Teresa breaks several ribs in a fall in Rome, is hospitalized for malaria, and undergoes surgery to clear a blocked blood vessel.

August 1996—Mother Teresa is hospitalized with malarial fever and failure of the left heart ventricle. She develops a lung infection and requires several additional hospital stays.

October 1996—President Bill Clinton makes Mother Teresa an honorary U.S. citizen.

March 1997—Sister Nirmala is elected as Mother Teresa's successor.

June 1997—Mother Teresa receives the Congressional Gold Medal of Honor.

September 1997—Mother Teresa passes away at her home in Calcutta after suffering a heart attack.

October 19, 2003—Mother Teresa is beatified in a celebration held by Pope John Paul II in St. Peter's Square at the Vatican. In order to reach beatification, one posthumous miracle must be proven. For being credited with the miraculous cure of a woman with a stomach tumor in India, Mother Teresa is now elevated to the status of Blessed Mother Teresa.